Learn the Guitar:

The 7 Day Breakdown

A guide to everything you need to know about playing the guitar.

Dallin Aston

TABLE OF CONTENTS

DAY 1
INTRODUCTION

Congratulations on taking your first step in learning the guitar and opening this book! You will find this journey challenging at times, but very rewarding.

Now, unfortunately there is not a magic button that you can press that will make you good, or a secret that will transform you into a master of the guitar overnight. Practice and consistency together will be the only way to get where you want to go and play the way you want to play.

In this book, we will walk through the very basics of the guitar. We will also cover tuning, posture, how to hold a pick, finger exercises, notation, tablature, scales, beginning theory, chords, strumming, and more!

As you begin this exciting new journey, try not to limit yourself to only one genre (style) of music. You will learn so much more by listening to Rock, Jazz, Blues, Classical, and Spanish styles of guitar. Spending time with other musicians and learning from their experience and knowledge can also be a huge help! Everyone possesses a different interpretation of music and songwriting, so welcome advice and tips from other musicians as often as you can!

Learning the guitar will enrich your life in many ways, but it can be frustrating as you first begin to play. Remember to always have fun. is to remember to have fun. If you are not having fun, it will be much harder to keep going. Try to be patient with yourself, no one expects you to pick up the guitar for the first time and magically be a pro. Enjoy being a beginner and learn as much as you can. Try to love the process, you'll look back years down the road and be glad you did.

FUNDAMENTALS OF THE GUITAR

The first step in your journey is to familiarize yourself with your guitar. Understanding the different parts of the guitar and the accessories you will need will be vital in unlocking your full potential. See figure 1 for a full run down on the parts of the guitar you need to know.

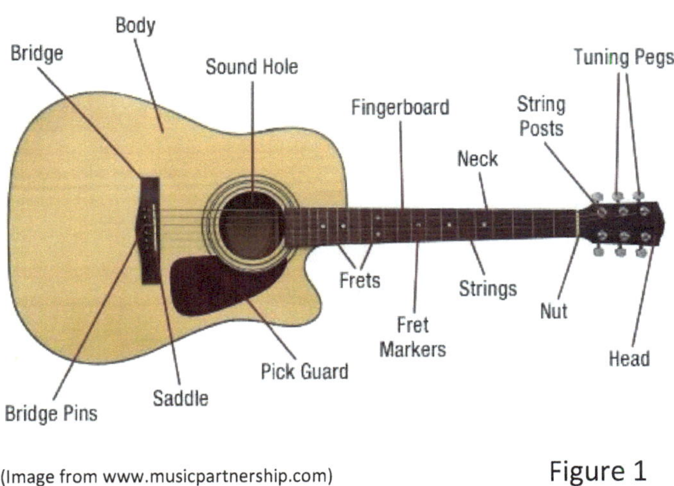

(Image from www.musicpartnership.com)   Figure 1

The Bridge area is the first part we will look at. The bridge is where strings are installed, bridge pins are what keep the strings in place, and the saddle is what the strings rest on to hover above the neck. Next we have the pick guard which protects the guitar from potential scratches as a result of strumming with a pick. The sound hole is where the actual sound escapes from the body after strings are played.

The neck of the guitar has a series of metal bars called frets, which are placed gradually closer together down the fretboard to increase the pitch of the note played. Fret markers allow you to easily know what fret you are playing and where you are on the fretboard.

It's important to know the six string names (From low to high: E A D G B E), especially when dealing with the head of the guitar. First you will find the nut, which holds the strings in place much like the saddle at the other end of the instrument. The string posts, like the bridge pins, keep the strings secure and the tuning pegs allow you to tighten the strings so you can tune up and sound great.

<u>Note</u>: Being able to string a guitar is an important skill to learn as a guitarist, so remember to make sure that you take careful note of which way you are threading the strings around the string posts. Try changing out only one string at a time to avoid confusion. You want 3 strings on the left side of the head to be wound the same direction and vice versa on the right.

Referring to figure 1, the top left tuning peg is for the Low E String, the top middle peg is for the A String, and the top right is for the D String. The bottom right peg is for the G String, the bottom middle is for the B String, and the bottom left is for the High E String.

TUNING

Learning to tune a guitar is vital in learning to master the instrument. There are several ways to tune up. Digital tuners, YouTube videos, and pianos or keyboards can all help you sound great, but there are also some cool tricks that will help you tune up and train your ear at the same time.

This method of tuning is called 5th fret tuning. Using a tuner or video to get the Low E string is important, but after that all you need is your guitar and your ear. After your Low E String is in tune, play the 5th fret of the Low E and you will get an A. This is because 5 steps up from E is A: E, F, F#, G, G#, A. If you remember the string names, the next string after the Low E String is an A. Therefore the 5th fret of the Low E is the same note as the A String, so they should sound the same. If they don't, just adjust the corresponding tuning peg. This principle can be used for to tune every string (except for the G String) as follows: The 5th fret of the A String should sound the same as the D String, the 5th fret of the D String should sound the same as the G String, the 4th fret of the G String should be the same as the B string, and finally the 5th fret of the B String should sound the same as the High E String.

Note: Remember to tune often, don't be afraid to tune multiple times during a practice session or performance. There is nothing worse than playing for someone only to be forced to stop mid song to retune. Tuning often will also help train your ear to hear when notes are and aren't in tune.

HAND AND FINGER BASICS

Playing the guitar requires the use of our hands and fingers in ways that aren't necessarily normal, especially if this is your first time picking up an instrument. It may be difficult at first, but that's okay! Here's what you need to know.

You have one fretting hand (which hand this is depends on if you are righthanded or left-handed. If you are right-handed, then your fretting hand will be your left hand.), which is the hand responsible for creating chords or single notes on the fretboard. Your other hand is your picking or strumming hand. Both are equally important and have unique roles in making music on the guitar.

Figure 2 shows your fretting hand (if you are right-handed) and how to refer to your fingers. This will be a great visual aid for building chords correctly and reading chord diagrams in the future.

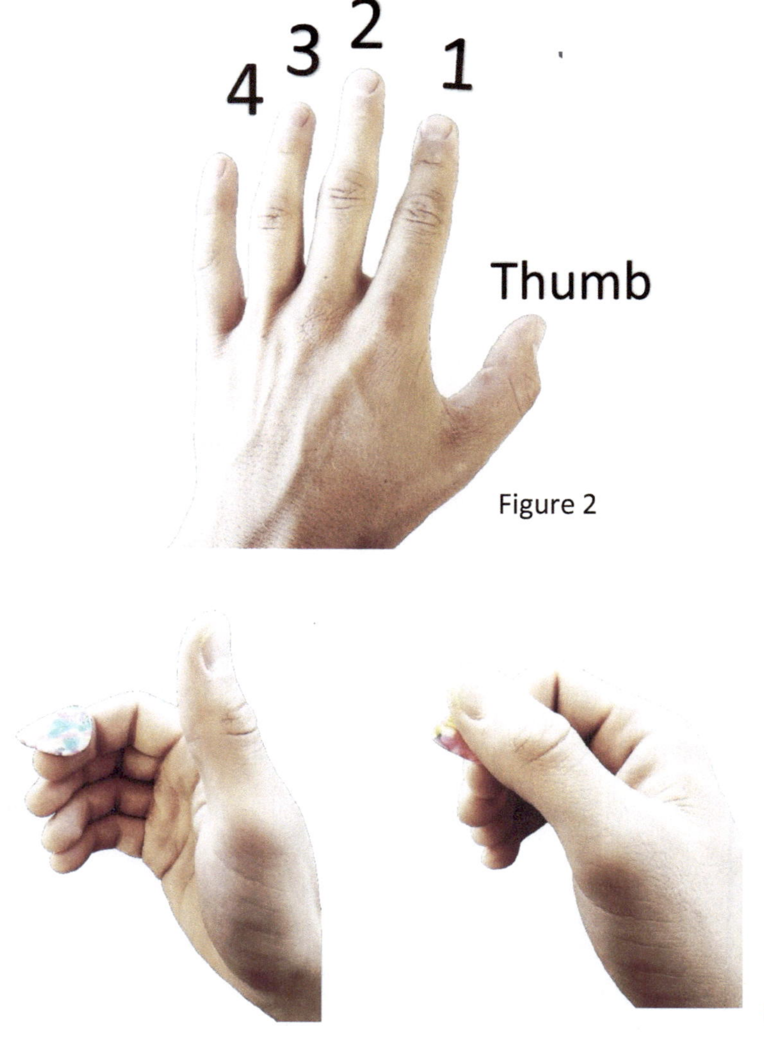

Figure 2

Figure 3

Figure 3 demonstrates your strumming hand and how to correctly hold a guitar pick. Lightly rest the pick between your thumb and forefinger. Your forefinger needs to be arched so that it forms a semi-circle. The pick will rest on the tip of your forefinger and from here you will place your thumb on the pick creating a loose yet stable pressure.

Most music stores sell tools to help exercise and strengthen your hands and fingers. There are, however, a lot of different ways to build strength and speed:

- Place your hand on a flat surface and lift one finger at a time. Go for accuracy first, and gradually build speed. Next, try lifting every other finger, and again, go for accuracy, then speed.

- Spread your fingers out and touch the center of your palm with each finger while keeping your other fingers as straight as possible. This will help with coordination. Go for accuracy, and then speed.

- Squeeze a tennis ball or racquet ball.

DAY 2

MAJOR CHORDS

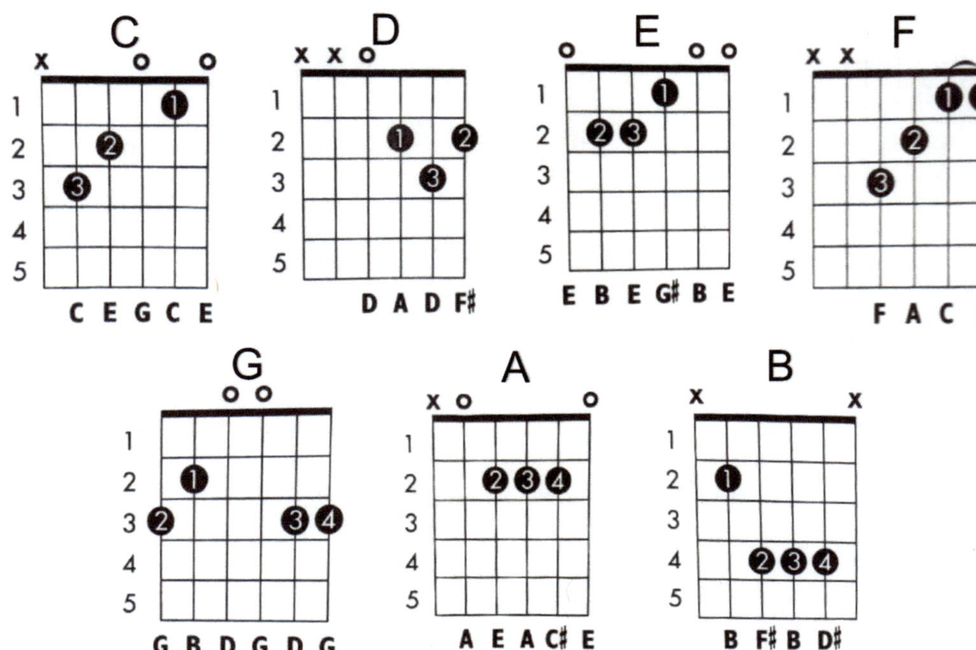

LEGEND: The numbers in the solid circles on the diagram represent which finger is placed where. Circles above the chart represent open strings. Xs represent a string or note not played (muted).

Each of these major chords are built from a corresponding major scale. We will go into beginning theory later. Each of these major chords also consists of a triad in notation. The formula for a major triad consists of R-3-5. This means that in the C major scale (C D E F G A B C), the Root is C, the 3rd is E, and the 5th is G. When you play a C major chord, the only notes strummed are C E G.

In the chord charts above, B and F are simplified, the normal chord formations are what are known as barre chords (which will be discussed later).

MINOR CHORDS

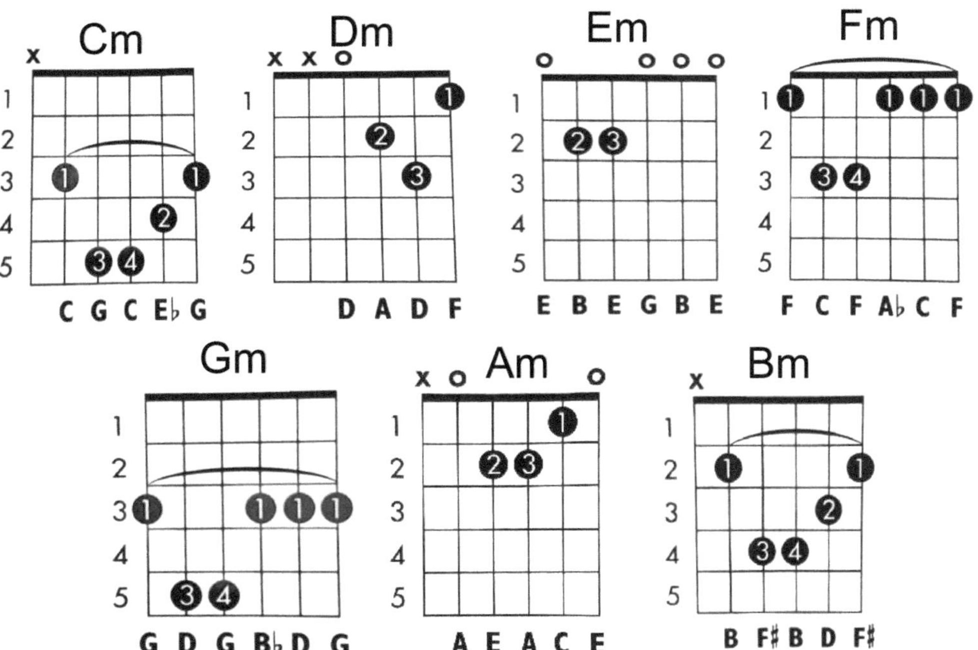

Like the major chords, minor chords are built from a corresponding minor scale. Each of the minor chords consists of a triad in notation. The formula for a minor triad is as follows: R-3♭(flatted)-5. This means that in the C minor scale (C D E♭ F G A♭ B♭ C), the root is C, the 3rd is Eb, and the 5th is G. Notice that it is the same as a major triad except for the flatted 3rd. Within the diagrams above, Cm, Fm, Gm, and Bm are all barre chords. This simply means that one finger holds down more than one string, indicated by the curved line across the diagram. Refer to Day 6 for more information.

DOMINANT 7ᵀᴴ CHORDS

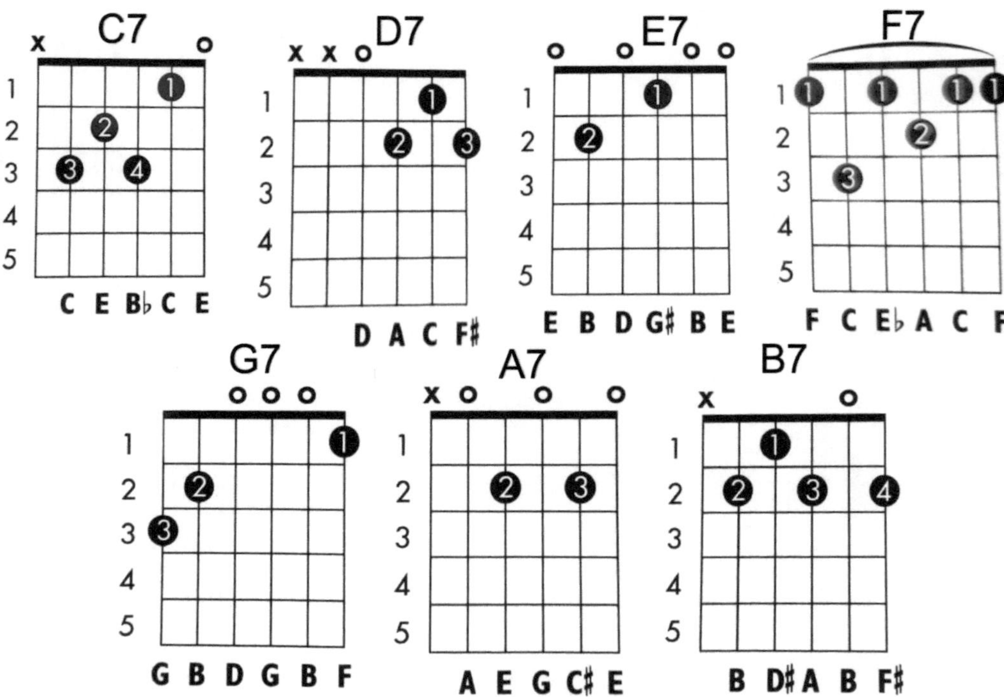

7th chord formations are a little different. The principles are still the same as a standard major chord formation, but the 7th note is added. The 7th note played in a 7th chord will be lowered ½ step. In the C Dominant 7th scale (C D E F G A B♭ C), the root is C, the 3rd is E, the 5th is G, and the 7th is B♭. The formula for this chord formation is R-3-5-7♭. If we have a four-note construct, a triad will still be the basic form in notation, but there will be an additional note, the 7th.

<u>Note</u>: For the F7 Chord, feel free to play only the bottom 4 strings. This chord can be challenging to play all 6 strings.

MAJOR 7TH CHORDS

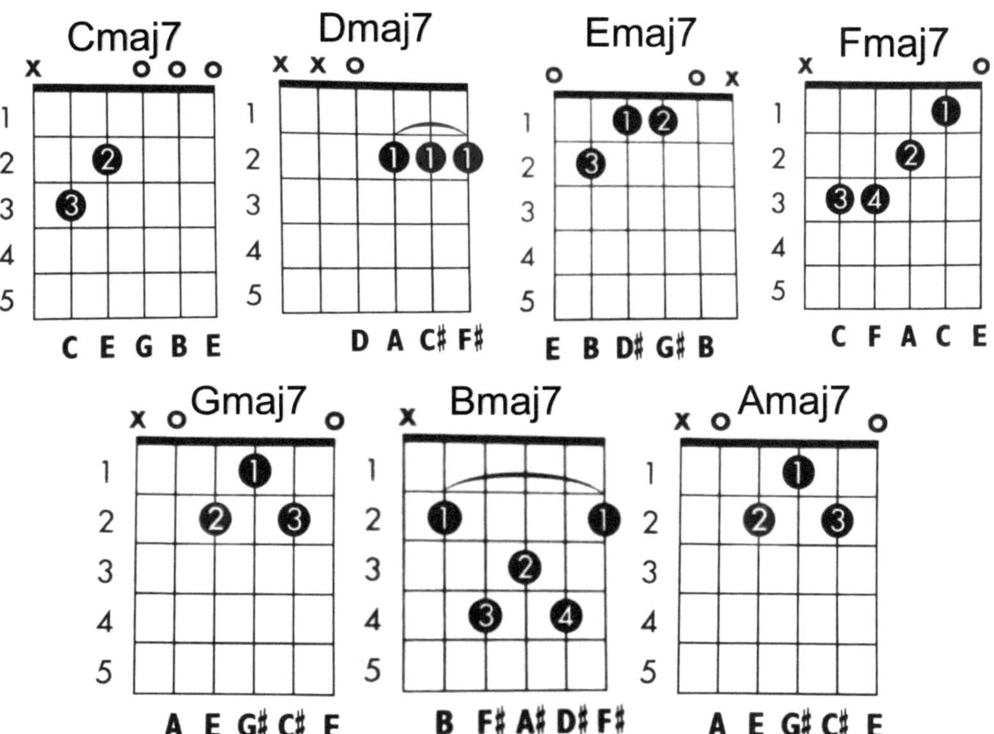

Major 7th chords are very similar to dominant 7th chords. The difference is that the major 7th follows the major scale identically. In the C major scale (C D E F G A B C), the root is C, the 3rd is E, the 5th is G, and the 7th is B. Notice that unlike the dominant 7th chord, the B is not flat.

MINOR 7TH OPEN CHORDS

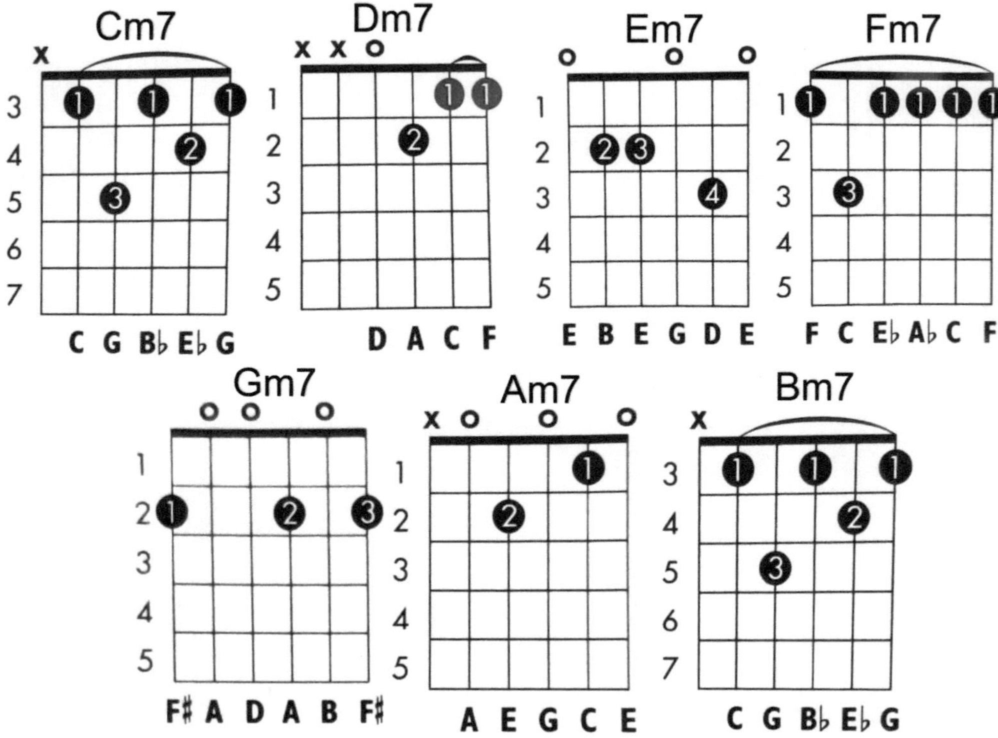

The minor 7th chord is just like the major 7th, only with the minor chord formation formula instead. In the C minor 7th scale, (C D Eb F G Ab Bb C), the root is C, the 3rd is Eb, the 5th is G, and the 7th is Bb. The formula for this chord is R-3b-5-7b. Just like the major 7th chord, a standard triad is built out of the R-3b-5, and the 7th tone is added.

ALTERNATE CHORDS

Now, it may sound daunting, but there are hundreds of chords out there. The good news is that it they all stem from the foundational chords we learned in this chapter.

Among the other alternate chords are diminished (A diminished chord consists of a R-3b-5b formula. It looks almost identical to the minor scale expect the 5th is also flatted. They are written with a o or dim) and augmented chords (An augmented chord is built R-3-5#. The 5th is sharp or raised ½ step. Augmented chords are written with a + sign next to the letter.)

SUMMARY ON CHORDS

Transitioning between chords can be frustrating, but with practice and patience, you will be playing in no time. Try to memorize how chords are build and engrave them into your muscle memory. Eventually you will simply be able to feel the chords on the fretboard.

DAY 3

BEGINNING THEORY

Music theory will give you a greater understanding of what you are playing and why, making music really fun!

Now that you have learned some strings, triads, and some chord formations, we are ready to dive in and start learning about music itself. Remember, learning basic theory may be a bit challenging, but it will make you a much better musician and guitarist.

Understanding theory and scales is a lot easier with something to look at so make sure you refer back to the image on the right in your efforts to learn how it all works!

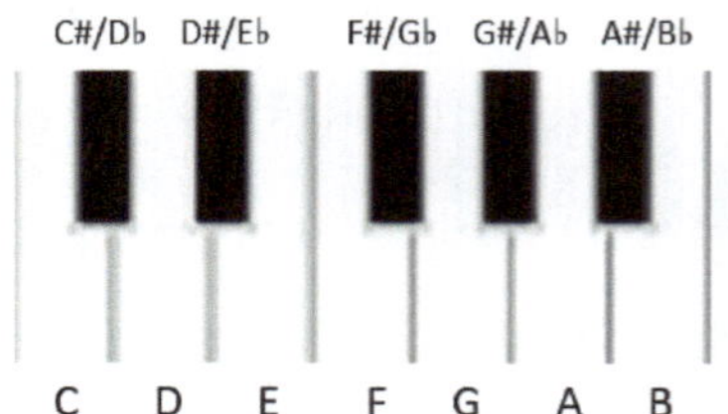

MAJOR SCALES

Before we begin with how to construct a major scale, know that there are only twelve notes in existence: C C#/Db, D, D#/Eb, E, F, F#/Gb, G, G#/Ab, A, A#/Bb, B, C. This is called a chromatic scale and it includes every note. A chromatic scale consists entirely of half steps. Take special note that there isn't an E#/Fb, B#/Cb, this is because those notes do not exist. A half step up from E is F and a half step up from B is C. C to C# is a half-step, C# to D is a half-step, D to D# is a half-step, etc.

A scale is comprised of whole (w) and half (h) steps. The term scale comes from the Latin word scala which means ladder. An easy way to remember this is that a scale climbs like a ladder of notes. If we use a C major scale as an example while referencing the chromatic scale, the major scale construct will be easier to understand. A scale is comprised of 8 steps which can be either whole or half steps.

<u>Example</u>: C D E F G A B C. C to D is a whole-step, D to E is a whole-step, E to F is a half-step, F to G is a whole-step, G to A is a whole-step, A to B is a whole-step, B to C is a half-step.

The major scale formula is: WWHWWWH.

MINOR SCALES

C Major Scale: C D E F G A B C (0 sharps, 0 flats)

G Major Scale: G A B C D E F# G (1 sharp: F#)

D Major Scale: D E F# G A B C# D (2 sharps: F#, G#)

A Major Scale: A B C# D E F# G# A (3 sharps: F#, G#, C#)

E Major Scale: E F# G# A B C# D# E (4 sharps: F#, G#, C#, D#)

B Major Scale: B C# D# E F# G# A# B (5 sharps: F#, G#, C#, D#, A#)

F# Major Scale: F# G# A# B C# D# E# F# (6 sharps: F#, G#, C#, D#, A#, E#)

C# Major Scale: C# D# E# F# G# A# B# C# (All sharp)

F Major Scale: F G A B♭ C D E F (1 flat: B♭)

B♭ Major Scale: B♭ C D E♭ F G A B♭ (2 flats: B♭, E♭)

E♭ Major Scale: E♭ F G A♭ B♭ C D E♭ (3 flats: B♭, E♭, A♭)

A♭ Major Scale: A♭ B♭ C D♭ E♭ F G A♭ (4 flats: B♭, E♭, A♭, D♭)

Db Major Scale: Db EbF Gb Ab Bb C Db (5 flats: Bb, Eb, Ab, Db, Gb)

Gb Major Scale: GbAb Bb Cb Db Eb F Gb (6 flats: Bb, Eb, Ab, Db, Gb, Cb)

Cb Major Scale: Cb Db Eb Fb Gb Ab Bb Cb (All flat)

MINOR SCALES

There are three different types of minor scales: natural, harmonic, and melodic. The formula above is for a natural minor scale. The difference between a natural and harmonic minor scale will be explained later.

A minor scale, like the major scale, consists of 8 steps - some whole steps and some half steps. The formula for a minor scale is: WHWWHWW.

C minor scale: C D Eb F G Ab Bb C

D minor scale: D E F G A Bb C D

E minor scale: E F# G A B C D E

F minor scale: F G Ab Bb C Db Eb F

G minor scale: G A Bb C D Eb F G

A minor scale: A B C D E F G A

B minor scale: B C# D E F# G A B

C# minor scale: C# D# E F# G# A B C#

Eb minor scale: Eb F Gb Ab Bb Cb Db Eb

F# minor scale: F# G# A B C# D E F#

G# minor scale: G# A# B C# D# E F# G#

Bb minor scale: Bb C Db Eb F Gb Ab Bb

HARMONIC MINOR SCALES

A harmonic minor scale builds off a natural minor scale. To play a harmonic minor, raise the 7th step of the scale by a ½ step. The formula for this scale is WHWWHWH.

C harmonic minor scale: C D Eb F G Ab B C

G harmonic minor scale: G A Bb C D Eb F# G

D harmonic minor scale: D E F G A Bb C# D

A harmonic minor scale: A B C D E F G# A

E harmonic minor scale: E F# G A B C D# E

B harmonic minor scale: B C# D E F# G A# B

F# harmonic minor scale: F# G# A B C# D E# F#

C# harmonic minor scale: C# D# E F# G# A B# C#

G# harmonic minor scale: G# A# B C# D# E FX(G) G#

Eb harmonic minor scale: Eb F Gb Ab Bb Cb D Eb

Bb harmonic minor scale: Bb C Db Eb F Gb A Bb

F harmonic minor scale: F G Ab Bb C Db E F

<table>
<tr><td>Example:</td></tr>
<tr><td>Natural Minor Scale: C D Eb F G Ab Bb C</td></tr>
<tr><td>Melodic Minor Scale: C D Eb F G Ab B C</td></tr>
</table>

<u>Note</u>: A double sharp simply indicates that you raise the note a whole step instead of a ½ step. As shown in the G# Harmonic Scale above, an FX is the same as a G. The same principle applies to a double flat. You would lower a note a whole step.

MELODIC MINOR SCALES

A melodic minor scale builds off both the natural and harmonic minor scales.

In music theory, a melodic minor scale is only used while ascending. When you go to descend, it switches back to a natural minor scale:

C D E♭ F G A B C C B♭ A♭ G F E♭ D C.

Example:

C Natural Minor Scale:

C D E♭ F G A♭ B♭ C C

Harmonic Minor Scale:

C D E♭ F G A♭ B C C

Melodic Minor Scale: C D E♭ F G A B C

NOTES ON THE FRETBOARD

Try your best to remember the notes on the fretboard, this will allow you to grow exponentially as a guitarist.

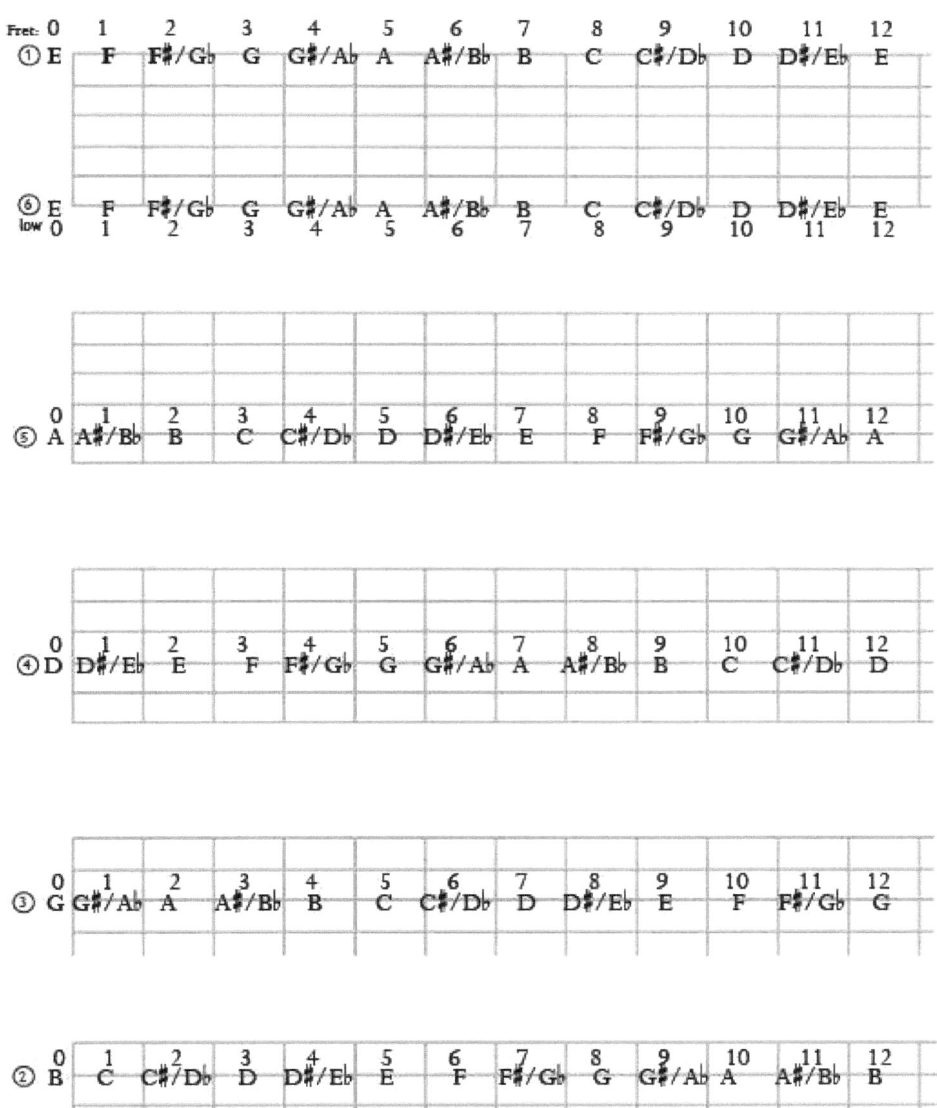

DAY 4

Beginning Theory Continued

KEY SIGNATURE GLOSSARY WITH CORRESPONDING MINORS

Key Signature	Added #	Major Key	Minor Key	Key Signature	Added ♭	Major Key	Minor Key
1 sharp	F#	G major	E minor	1 flat	B♭	F major	D minor
2 sharps	C#	D major	B minor	2 flats	E♭	B♭ major	G minor
3 sharps	G#	A major	F# minor	3 flats	A♭	E♭ major	C minor
4 sharps	D#	E major	C# minor	4 flats	D♭	A♭ major	F minor
5 sharps	A#	B major	G# minor	5 flats	G♭	D♭ major	B♭ minor
6 sharps	E#	F# major	D# minor	6 flats	C♭	G♭ major	E♭ minor
7 sharps	B#	C# major	A# minor	7 flats	F♭	C♭ major	A♭ minor

Key Signatures: (Refer to the diagram above) Flat key signatures will indicate which note(s) are flat. Sharp key signatures will indicate which note(s) are sharp.

NOTATION AND OTHER MUSIC SYMBOLS

While tablature is the most common form of written guitar music, learning to read musical notation is a valuable skill to have as a musician and guitarist. We will go into tablature on Day 5, but the following is a brief explanation of notation and how to read it:

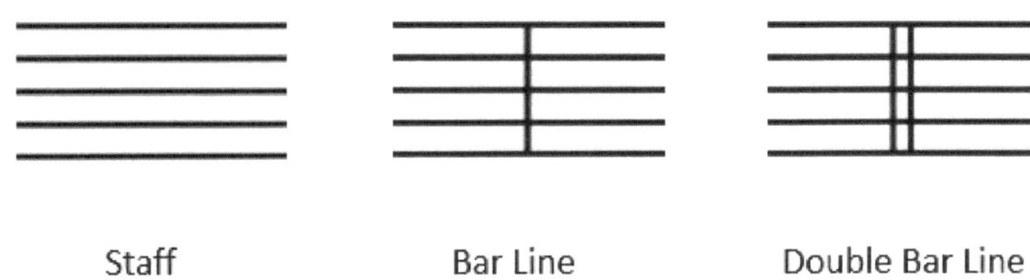

Staff   Bar Line   Double Bar Line

Staff: This is the set of lines upon which notes are placed. Beginning from the bottom line and continuing to the top, notes read differently depending on what clef is used. (A clef is explained below)

Bar Line: Bar lines are used to separate measures in a musical piece.

Double Bar Line: A double bar line is used to separate to major sections of music inside a piece. They may be used at a tempo change or key change.

Treble Clef   Bass Clef

Treble Clef: G clef is derived from the stylized G shape of the clef and the fact that the inside spiral circles the G line on the staff. The Treble clef is used for higher notes.

Bass Clef: The bass clef is also known as the F clef. The line in-between the 2 dots is an F note, hence the other name. It is for lower notes.

<u>Note</u>: There are other clefs known as the alto and tenor clefs. (These, however are not generally used in guitar music. They are very frequently used however, in other forms of music.)

Specific Time	Common Time	Cut Time

Specific Time: The bottom number refers to the kind of note that gets the count. The top number indicates how many of those notes you will find in a measure. In this case, the 4 represents quarter notes, and the 3 shows that there will be 3 quarter notes per measure. This is also referred to as three-four time. This will vary from piece to piece.

Common Time: Common time is used to represent 4/4 time. It indicates that there are 4 quarter notes per measure.

Cut Time: Cut time is just like it sounds. It represents 2/2 time. There are 2 quarter notes per measure.

Whole Note	Half Note	Quarter Note

Whole Note: A whole note gets four beats. In 4/4 time, only one whole note would be played making up the entire measure.

Half Note: A half note gets two beats. In 4/4 time, two half notes would be played in a measure.

Quarter Note: A quarter note gets one beat. In 4/4 time, four notes would be played in a measure.

Eighth Note	Sixteenth Note	Thirty-second Note	Sixty-fourth Note

Eighth Note: An eighth note receives a half beat. In 4/4 time, eight notes would be played per measure.

Sixteenth Note: A sixteenth note receives a quarter of one beat. In 4/4 time, sixteen notes would be played per measure.

Thirty-Second Note: A thirty-second note receives a sixteenth of one beat. In 4/4 time, thirty-two notes would be played per measure.

Sixty-Fourth Note: A sixty-fourth note receives one thirty-second of one beat. In 4/4 time, sixty-four notes would be played per measure.

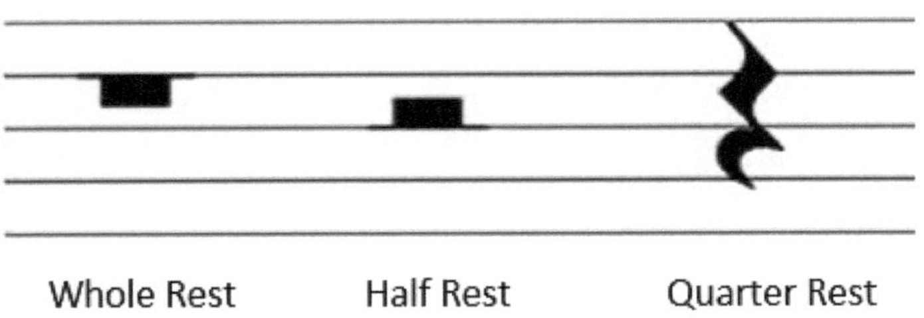

Whole Rest   Half Rest   Quarter Rest

Whole Rest: A whole rest gets 4 counts. In 4/4 time, it would receive 4 counts per measure.

Half Rest: A half rest gets 2 counts. In 4/4 time, it would receive 2 counts per measure.

Quarter Rest: A quarter rest gets 1 count. In 4/4 time, it would receive 1 count per measure.

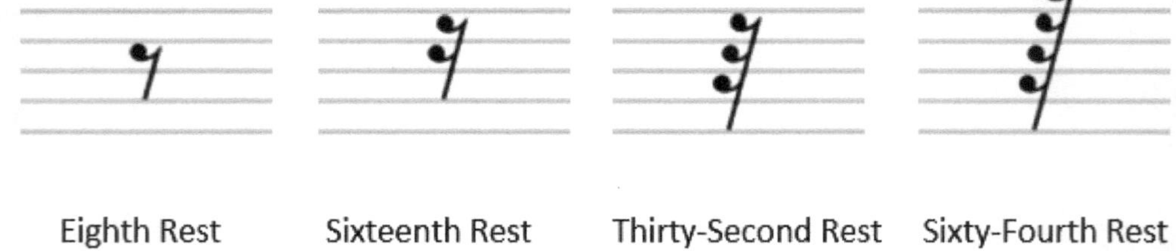

Eighth Rest   Sixteenth Rest   Thirty-Second Rest   Sixty-Fourth Rest

Eighth Rest: An eighth rest receives a half beat. In 4/4 time, eight beats would be contained in each measure.

Sixteenth Rest: A sixteenth rest receives a quarter of one beat. In 4/4 time, sixteen beats would be contained in each measure.

Thirty-second Rest: A thirty-second rest receives a sixteenth of one beat. In 4/4 time, thirty-two beats would be contained in each measure.

Sixty-fourth Rest: A sixty-fourth rest receives one thirty-second of one beat. In 4/4 time, sixty-four beats would be contained in each measure.

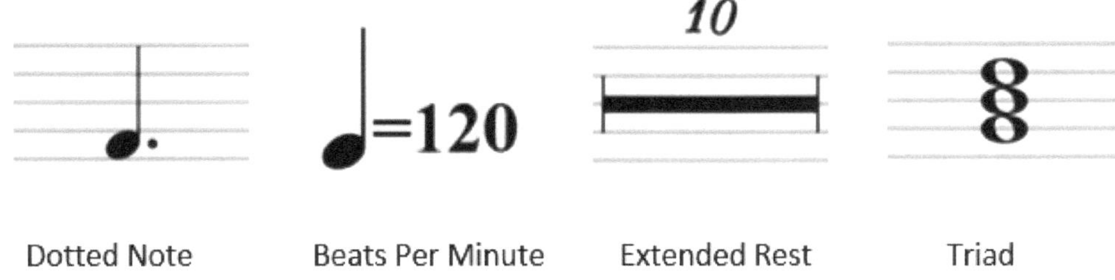

| Dotted Note | Beats Per Minute | Extended Rest | Triad |

Dotted Note: Placing a dot to the right of any note value lengthens the value by one half its value. A dot can also be placed to the right of a rest causing the same to happen - increased value. For example, a dotted quarter note would get 1 and a half beats.

Beats Per Minute: This indicates how many quarter notes will occur in one minute. A metronome can help you understand tempo and set the beats per minute. A metronome is a piece of equipment that keeps time. You can buy this at a music store, or you can get a metronome app that also works great.

Extended Rest: An extended rest will cover more than just a specific amount of time inside a measure. It will be for the indicated number of measures. In the case above, it is 10 measures of rest.

Triad: This is a picture of what a triad looks like. It is simply a collection of 3 notes together, and we have spent quite a bit of time talking about how to build one.

SUMMARY ON THEORY

Remember, no one expects you to become a master on theory simply after reading this chapter. This lesson is here to help you build on your current skills so that your knowledge expands while you practice chords and scales. A comprehensive understanding of what you are playing and why it is the way it is will take you far in your endeavors.

DAY 5

TABLATURE

What is tablature? Tablature, tab for short, is a form of musical notation with an emphasis on fingerings rather than traditional notation. Tablature is commonly used for fretted instruments such as the guitar.

The problem with tablature is that it doesn't indicate note length or duration. This is where understanding note values will help, as most tablature is written below standard notation.

Tablature is a closer visual representation of your guitar fretboard, thereby making it easier to interpret music. It doesn't require much training at all to become fluent.

Below is a sample of what guitar tablature looks like and how to read it. Remember, tablature will be read upside down in comparison to how the strings are on your guitar. <u>Note</u>: The bottom line of the tab is the Low E string.

- 0 represents an open string and the number represent which finger is used to play what.

- The number stacked on top of each other represents the strumming of a chord.

- An x represents a muted string.

- The curved line connecting the two notes represents a pull off, which is when a note is picked and then one of your fingers on your fretting hand pulls off the string to the next note behind it sounding the note.

- An h represents a hammer on, which is where one note is played and your finger hammers onto a higher fret to produce the sound instead of your picking hand.

- A slide is represented by the slash in-between the two numbers and is done by sliding your finger from one fret to another.

- The wave looking symbol represents a bend, which is simply bending the string so that the pitch goes higher while keeping your finger on the same fret.

DAY 6

CAGED SYSTEM FOR BARRE CHORDS

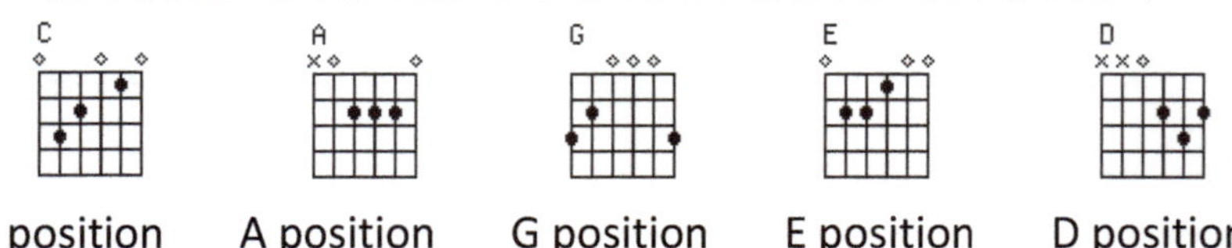

The caged system is simple, it involves the five positions above as they are considered movable. If you start with an open E chord, you can slide that position up one fret and barre with your first finger (You will also have to adjust your finger positions accordingly). Once you have barred the first fret and moved the E position up one fret, you have a new chord: F major (this is a barre chord, which is simply a chord that requires multiple notes to be pressed by the same finger). You can do this all the way up the fret board chromatically. Once you have hit the 12th fret, you are at an octave higher E chord.

If your chord begins in the 2nd fret (such as A, D, G), there will be a one fret space between the barre and the chord formation. Each of the formations can be moved up the fretboard chromatically, and each of the chords are an octave higher at the 12th fret. Chords B major and F major are extensions of the E and A chord forms.   Here are some examples of this system:

A FORM

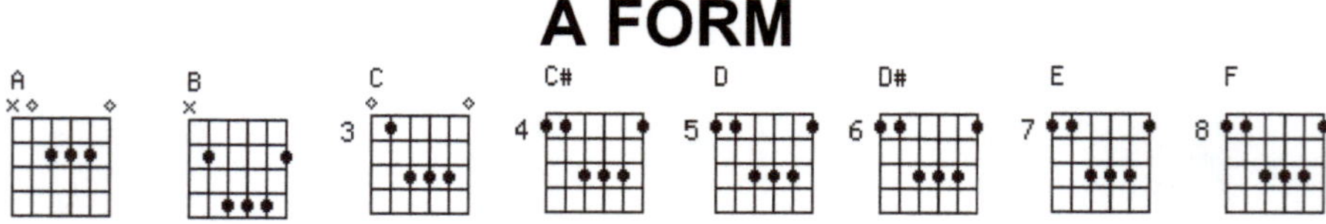

E FORM

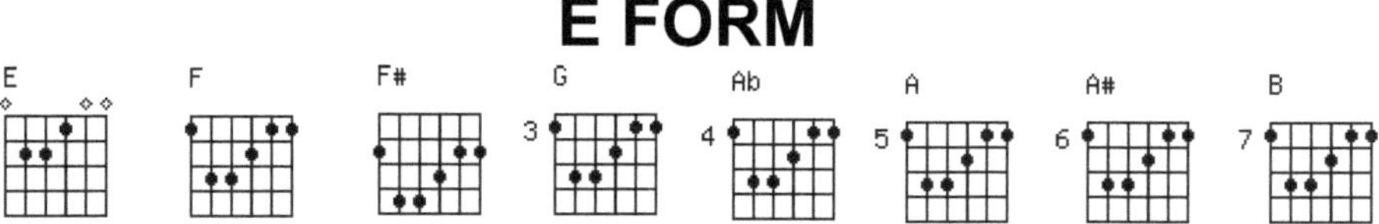

POWER CHORDS

Power chords are different than other chords because rather than including R-3-5, a power chord is simply R-5. Below are some examples of power chords. A lot of modern rock songs use power chords, and they are very common. They are much simpler and sound great.

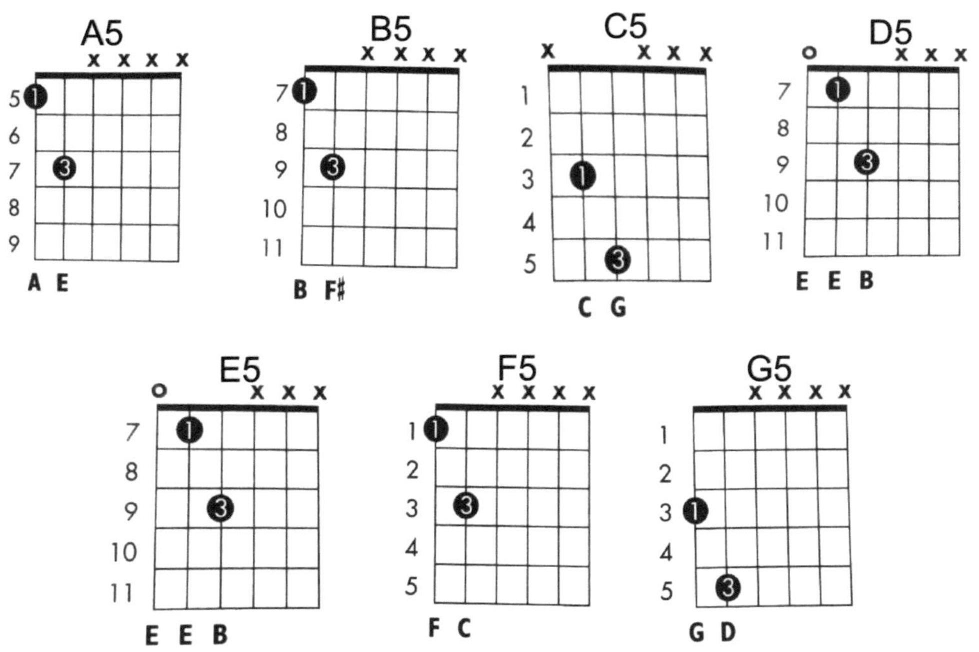

STRUMMING PATTERNS

Strumming the guitar can be a challenge as you get started in making all the notes in a chord ring out or getting the strumming pattern right and in rhythm, but all of this will get better with time and practice. A lot of new guitarists want to strum the strings too hard and some use their whole arm to strum instead of just their wrist.

- Be sure to hold your pick correctly and not too tight or too loose.
- In a downward motion, lightly glide the pick over your strings.
- Don't try and strum too fast at first; go for accuracy and then speed.
- Practice strumming whole notes, half notes, quarter notes, eighth notes, and sixteenth notes.
- Practice using a down/up pattern.
- Strum with your wrist, not your arm.

As far as actual patterns are concerned, most strumming is unique to the song you are playing. Some strumming patterns will be indicated by D (down) and U (up) symbols. Some will be indicated by / (down) and \ (up), and some will be indicated by actual note values where there will be a combination of whole, half, quarter, eighth, and sixteenth notes.

DAY 7

TIME TO PLAY

Picking a song that you actually want to learn is far more enjoyable than being forced to play songs not of your choosing. Refer to the information in this book often and play at least a little bit every day. If you want to be great at something, you must do it daily.

CONCLUSION

Congratulations, you have made it to the end of this book! But don't worry, your journey playing the guitar has only just begun!

As stated at the beginning of Day 1, playing the guitar can be challenging, but it can also be very rewarding! The best thing to do is to develop good habits. This will save you lots of trouble in the future. Take your time and learn theory, scales, tab and the fretboard well. Practice chord changes and progressions until you know them like the back of your hand. Try different chord progressions, avoid getting stuck into playing the same 4 chords over and over again, and don't be afraid to sing the chords to yourself while you learn.

Most importantly, relax when you play and have a good time! There's a lot to know, and it's not going to happen overnight, but if you put your heart into it, you'll be playing like a pro in no time!